SEARCHER

Copyright 2008 Johnny Arbogast

All rights reserved. No part of this book may be reproduced without the express written consent of the author, except in the case of brief excerpts in critical reviews and articles. All inquiries should be addressed to:

Johnny Arbogast
johnnyarbogast@gmail.com

Cover Art by Campbell Z. Alexander

Chatanuga Café originally appeared in OSIRIS, Deerfield, MA

Convictions I Never Had originally appeared in SHOCK'S BRIDGE, Berkely, CA

Lac Du Bois originally appeared in STRAIGHT AHEAD, La Habra, CA

Flowers Limp From The Stem; *Beauty*; *Home Is Where The Toast Is*; *Happy*; and *Life With LouLou No. 1* originally appeared in THE MOMENT, Los Angeles, CA

ISBN 978-0-6152-3785-5

SEARCHER

Collected Poems, 1988 – 2008

By Johnny Arbogast

~~ film or reality
Love is something awaited ~~

Table of Contents

Chatanuga Café	3
Flowers Limp From the Stem	4
Home is Where the Toast Is	6
Convictions I Never Had	7
Beauty	8
Lac Du Bois	9
Happy	10
14 Lives With LouLou	11
Like Legs	31
The Secret Valet	32
Emotion	33
Papers	35
Of Corsican	36
Maelstrom	38
Always the Charmer	39
Swan's Song	40
A New Hope	41
If My Heart Could Beat	42
The Goddess Factor	43
I'll Never Be Cured*	46
My Every Effort	47
I Should Shut Up	49
The Searchers	51
I Know	52
Hopelessly	53

~Continued~

Goddess Days Afar	55
Folding Chair	56
Desires	58
Every moment	59
Crazy Ass Missing You	60
Chemolithoautotrophic Hyperthermophiles	62
Blackberry December	64
An Universal Wolf	66
Beautiful and Wonderful	67
A Tendency, A Tendency	68
Your Sister Falls Asleep With the T.V. On	69
Hostage Situation	70
Appearances	71
Blue	74
Crime	78
Afterword	81

SEARCHER
1988 -2008

CHATANUGA CAFÉ

It's no wonder she sat there
I would have too
The warmth of the sun
In which to write a letter

It was late in the afternoon
But I was early
To huddle over foreign coffee
Watching her write

Her pen in right, cigarette in left
I know she hails, and mourns
My unknown brother or lover,
Mother or friend

And Smoking in the sunlight
She lends credence to faces
Dreams and filmy recollections
Pausing to gaze through the window

An hour later, after she's left
I imagine her on a walk
With me, dropping the letter
In a blue box to be forgotten

FLOWERS LIMP FROM THE STEM
Robert Duncan, 1919 - 1988

It will be early
    In the morning
The heaters racing the sun
    Voices on the radio
Subdued

It will crawl down the street
    Empty, wet with night rain
It will shout out in verse
    Echoing across the Bay
    Tremulous ideas and incantations
Scaling the currents
    Like flat rocks thrown

"If I only had one eye
I would see the empty glass
If I had lost a hand
I'd touch you soft
And only one ear would listen
The heart stilled"

~Continued~

It will never be angry
    Nor seemingly partial
Be calling
    Persistent
It will pierce a mother's wrist
    And later claim the son

It will be a slowly warming dream
    Beneath the bridge
    Around the island

HOME IS WHERE THE TOAST IS

The bus was on time
And I was home
(Home is where you're always welcome?)

I'm not who you think,
Shuffling through your world,
A sometime silent insanity
Can you smell the dried whiskey?
Your skin clammy,
Ghosts of long dead dreams.
You see the excavation of defeat;
Another violent hit and run,
Leaving only crippled smiles.

Three weeks this time,
Our first words unpleasant
(Home is where they tell you the truth.)

CONVICTIONS I NEVER HAD

What can you see?
Standing in another house
Do you wonder too…?
In these agnostic days
Our technological voices, crying of distance
Gentle please and promises
Born and travelled in the dial tone

Where am I tomorrow
Trying to say my name
Do we pass in the skies, I hope
(I dreamt of Simone and Jean-Paul, sitting
The April sun warming their faces)

Or maybe deep in the woods
Where solitude carries naked thoughts
Far away from our concrete allure
(We breathed late winter, one night
Beneath the moon at Quincy Market)

BEAUTY

What cries the dog forgotten
In the night of martyrs
His attested madness in ever
Tangling, earthly inferno
Or a single star perfect
Claiming relief of the infinite
Saved of desecration, unable
To see or feel, knowing
Self echoes
As seldom sung truth.
Tomorrow yields more
The mewling infants of destruction
Skin pink health and dread
And life, innocence in pain the
Witches cannot lie, helpless
Speaking the day no more past
Than will come troubled.
The bars cast their shadows true
Cold iron veins that do not pulse
This liberty of fate, they slat
And rhyme in black
This perplexion of placement.

LAC DU BOIS

It sure came as a surprise
On a
Long
Cold afternoon
In northern Minnesota
Everyone who knew
Me
Knew,

I'd finally turned into a squirrel

HAPPY

You can always get a table
Buttered bread
And a small glass of juice

We crawl
Each morning grappling
And though our senses are beneath the sea
The noise is like incredible chow mein

All nine windows
Spill the island light

FOURTEEN LIVES WITH LOULOU

NUMBER ONE

LouLou's bathing strange, not crying
So bright white, shining under dark
In the porcelain scrubbing queer
Not looking, never looking near
My face is somber
As she's fondly soaking, naked wet
Almost delicious fairly too spiced
Racy beautiful Southern France

LouLou's bathing madly ever
Slipping, splash, dripping
Off my heart
There's no more soap; un-penned
Memories fleeting rare
Some cagey old buzzards flying
Circles through the skull
Our silence solid bones broken

LouLou's bathing insane again
Pink and black plastic flowers
On her head, sealing away
Geysers, eruptions: her hair
Already scathing this morning
Splshing, rubber duck about her breast
Without too many words
Hurling mortally raping asides

~Continued~

LouLou's bathing lasting folly pure
Leaning back nose above weapons
Stilled at last surviving last
Would she never get out
Wrapping, covering, svelte purple
Towel dry, unconcerned
Or float away laughing
Away from herself, away laughing

NUMBER TWO

LouLou's smoking opium black
On the floor she's disguised
Like an old brown quilt
Part of her image fighting through
Moth-eaten, unemotional she's softer
Her eyes oily wandered, two blackened
Fish gone, nodding seas wondering

She's whispering to herself
"Left, then right again"
Nothing more just four less

LouLou's smoking in Southeast Asia
Ancient and doll faced, she's there
Cross-legged and binding hard, tight
Rules and films of her own device
Sometimes wicked, a curved knife
Preparing me
Making ready the needle and thread

So softly she's moaning
Crawling down the floor into suspension
"I've no more naked abilities"

~Continued~

LouLou's smoking around tables
Kissing the bottles of water, melting
Such slow softly glowing licking flames
Like her hands, clutching and firm
She doesn't see really
Reading in Braille raised by abuse
Casual, modern woman in ages today

NUMBER THREE

LouLou's happy at the Northern beach
Running, sand kicked behind
Chasing seagulls, wild hair
Ripping like red claws

LouLou's happy up to her ankles
In the always icy water
Jumping and dancing
Screaming in *joie de vivre*

(I reached for the moon
Tattooed along her belly)

LouLou's happy 'til the sun goes down
Like her, burning and fierce
Off the end of Earth, time
Trailing, winding down below the rocks

NUMBER FOUR

LouLou's cooking dinner sexy
Undetermined noises emerging
The kitchen cluttered and steamy
She's wearing an apron, whiter
Than the skin behind her knees
Soups and sauces like war paint
Streaking her cheeks

LouLou's cooking dinner not hungry
Flour and sugar drifting in air
Our first snowfall dry
Remarkable dusting on shoulders bare
She's muttering at dishes
Robustly alive in a city unfound

LouLou's cooking dinner resolute
Not ever pleading, she's warm and secure
The artificial igloo of the kitchen
Secure from this dark-green winter
No longer trembling or afraid
Working or playing with lascivious ingredients
Not an afterthought to an evening meal

NUMBER FIVE

LouLou's burning photo's flagrant
Abused black market baby erasing past
Present fears so bold, like mine
She advertizes her mania, scowling black
Etching permanence into hardwood floors
Crawling, dancing primal
Egyptian potency through the smoke

LouLou's burning, raging red
Splitting, writhing real, rolling
Sacred music loving tormenting inner
Waters never resting
She's bleeding distress, of no force
As the moons are rising
Deftly poured is the potion

LouLou's burning all the trees
Whole forests bare between
She's craving heat, sucking desperate
Athena striking back
The man above, defeated and humble
A meteor wailing faster
Startled but straight-footed ever

NUMBER SIX

LouLou's in time, stepping light
Forward a spell, crafty…

(Lately I can't see
Bumping into things
Lost in haze)

LouLou's in tiny seats, squeezing
Her ring-bedazzling unfortunate on hands

(She touched my knee
Gentle, eternities
Dusting in a brush)

LouLou's in painted cups beneath
The rim, falling drips of amber

(A brighter laugh tomorrow
Perhaps more pleasant
A new shade)

NUMBER SEVEN

LouLou's drinking a beer rare
Across red glass tables separating
Beautiful, reflecting powdery lines
Black, all black into depth

LouLou's drinking teas of sadness
Lacquered many layers onto souls
In the impetus of the night
Rocketry running away on Friday quests

LouLou's drinking airs and howls
Struggling brave on cliff
She's keeping secrets schematic
Driftwood she'll shape and revitalize

(I know I've watched her before
Spellbinding from surface inward
In thousands of individual jewels)

LouLou's drinking wine unwilling
Intemperance motionless, fervent, still
And she's by the hand, accompaniment gilded
Wafting into Algerian nights

~Continued~

LouLou's drinking juices before dawn
Solidifying images escaping unencumbered
Rumpled sheets white
In foredawn health and eloquence

LouLou's drinking drops from lashes above
She's brand new, perpetually manifest
In showers and childhood rhymes
With blackened soft ropes shaking

NUMBER EIGHT

LouLou's hiding in other clothes
Somewhere south on Easter
She's smiling in pills and banter
In theaters dark and illicit

LouLou's hiding in a vault, sneaking
Like art, for a second look sees more
Peeling a Birch, astonishment anew
In light and people, she's knowing

(We've our secret
Erotic and beautiful
Black
In watercolors
Ornamenting pieces recalling
The shore in softer grey
The beaches we'd walk
A trickle of wine
Polishing the owl's night
LouLou…)

NUMBER NINE

I hear their whimpers from my bed

    Drifting through the barely sterile walls
    The black stockings spread high
    In the corner, breathing slowly

I hear their whimpers in my misery

    Really sad, away from LouLou exploding
    On the floor, intrepid dark commando
    Sketching me, honed razor lines

I hear their whimpers echoing quickly

    Drawn true into her, inhaling
    Also dreams of droughty lofts in brick
    Other cities east and south away

I hear their whimpers and they are mine

    Lost and lonesome at every missed ring
    Telephones and wedding bands, her
    Fingers stroking, scratching blood

NUMBER TEN

She's ghostly mourning behind me

> A dark lean cat flashing
> Eyes, lightening electric alive
> Not crying for something else

She's ghostly mourning in night vision inky

> Floating through streets off beat
> She haunts and taunts to follow
> Groaning, reaching 'round blind

She's ghostly mourning stolen indulgence

> From pockets different, drugged
> Crazy red wine sex husband, behind
> Locked doors in sultry sheets moonlit

She's ghostly mourning Athena's shadow

> Flattered in the murky criss-cross
> Deftly moving, stepping precise confused
> Resting her head, weary, I think softly

NUMBER ELEVEN

She's out there sleeping, I know

She's out there breathing stately

She's out there away, I see the street

She's out there drifting, my cumulous

NUMBER TWELVE

(LouLou you're bold, I say
Admiring, warmed by your
Glance, I love you, I guess
LouLou, all the time here
And there, across the table,
Touching hands beneath, and
Across the city, my repose
To yours unfitted, these are
My tears of joy at minutes
In your arms, and fear
That you could ever cease, me
Striving always to bathe lovely,
Again LouLou, it's what's believed)

NUMBER THIRTEEN

LouLou's my baby, spoon-fed meals
With eyes so mournfully endearing
Almost crying, begging, saying
Secrets kept behind gallery doors

LouLou's my baby in the mornings
Rare sunlight to shower in, golden
Sundrops, teardrops to dampen
Rigid poses and postures grim

LouLou's my baby in danger perhaps
Not yet cut (like my nightmares)
Exposed to the same flames and anguish
Feeling her heart in fear, helpless

LouLou's my baby dear, sweet baby's
Shoulders to be stroked and smiles
To be induced fortunate breathy
Blending in black, bleeding her charm

NUMBER FOURTEEN

(I'm so mixed up LouLou
Some Brie on wonder bread
Some heroin and pink white
Wine, for lunch it feels like,
The days are spinning soft)

This spring in San Francisco, bright…

    North Beach is exotic, hands held
    In narrow streets, hunting
    Down that minestrone Old World
    Stretching in freedom of shadows

This spring impossible beautiful black…

    (I'd pull on my favorite tie
    And supper grand a sexy dark
    Time, I'd doff my hat as a
    Gentleman in any case, all
    Days sailing some distant bay)

LIKE LEGS

A perfect moment is believed
From the flat ink deepening
And it feels like someone's eye
Is missing. Tuesday, or any other
That has the early too bright,
The thoughts are unbelievable –
An abandoned bridge house this ghost

With whiskey colored hair.
The moon cuts a swatch triangular,
The point begins in the water
With a constantly moving, electric
Blue alphabet.
It grows thicker stretching out
Past the black relief boats that

Shift just slightly.
Her bones such a spare sculpture,
Like a late night confession that
Shouldn't have been made
But has become a hinge
And simple honesty and caring
Swing with confusing release.

THE SECRET VALET:
Or why I shot myself in the foot

I look after the old
Woman
Who had babies
And divorced
A race car driver.
I find taxies
Pour champagne
In the evening,
My keeping
For the children are
Grown away
And her Russian old man
Works.
She sells art
And talks of
Too many experiences
She buys new clothes, has her
Hair done
Keeps herself up –
Reads Tolstoy.

EMOTION

Begin like a soul secret desire:
Sex running kinky ruining control,
It's just like imagination
Filled with hit and run designs
Always late at night and so high octane,
It transforms all the mundane staging
And books move away quickly, they are
Disfigured, but the words ram the senses.
Mothers don't understand the need, for
Booze and pills and wine, they move around
But never about control or pacing; just
Don't say it or come in close contact.

Then becoming what was screamed and wailed:
A head is pounded out endlessly
Or beaten as with ordinary tools,
Ugly maybe, it seems untouched but the lumps
Do rise. They convey the way rocks are passed
On unpaved roads or bowels in turmoil.
See, God is unthinkable when
Standing knee deep in this dark refuse.
Later, drums are heard from ship to ship,
Flight is over anything and anything must
Be green or dying of what was once
Suggestion only, pure and unstepped on.

~Continued~

Finally a killer on the road and ever:
All alone with organs of infestation rising,
Crowning and breaking up the clouds,
Beneath a moon along a shore.
Women and flowers contrived, cut-outs from
A daily newspaper glued to the frequent
Ruminations and tawdry studio flat walls.
What's visual should never be seen.
Statistics are the undoing, belying tenets, like
A granny's kiss, a false saint of superstition and
Fear. Emotion is a profession or so it seems.

PAPERS

… sure buddy, said the man in the
truck, and gimme a light too.
hammer down, runnin' down, he ran
through the next town, screeching
at the edge as he just missed a female
terrorist standing in the road, m-16 at
ease. you should do this for a
living, he said almost to himself while
searching through trash on the dash
(for what? he didn't find it).
the nose pointed sharply into the
hole at the end of the highway;
the man reached into the back,
into a cooler on the seat there, and
came back dripping, with cans of beer.
two quick snaps. a couple of hours,
he said, port st. lucie in a couple of hours…

OF CORSICAN

October should never end, my one time self
Swampy days would traipse forever, couldn't leap
Away from the Fall, a drooling, vile elf.
Into the balance thrown – little peep –
How could a self ignore this price quite steep?
Finally pretty Elba earns her drizzle,
Sputters, but process cannot fizzle.

Amnesia is a sure, yet feeble out…
There's a bucket for these rags of dull grey.
No antiquated notion! People shout,
Chatting through phone, execution or stay?
Able was a self, espy a lonely way.
These new waters hard as a painted wall,
Pounding out sounds of the saddest squall.

Happy anniversary and all that rot,
A self on the path, kicking through the leaves.
Horrible recounting of what's been brought:
The armies are lost, Josephine grieves,
Self shouts, forgive me, late under the eaves.
Conjour up thoughts, *fleur de lis* and roses,
A defeated adventurer dozes.

~Continued~

Self crime: the trial, the ache persuasive.
Conjugating verbs alone, smoky dreams –
Years spent holding hands at tables pensive,
Eyes are now honed, volumes of cobra screams.
Unfortunately, it's just what it seems.
A later sea air breathes rotten news,
Self slapped, self beaten, little left to lose.

Crossing waters, think revisiting done.
Landed self, sea legs walk to drink wassail,
To extract from sin and create some fun.
But scenarios sit, will they prevail?
Self recriminations begin travail.
Humor is codeine, red wine brought by boat:
Sizzle sot self! It's really just a moat.

Surprised self, an ungodly charmer
Realizing slick skating over black ice.
Cold nightmares, in the hole, must not harm her,
Caught away, the people suspecting vice
Echo on empty island, out think twice
Caged wonder shown about, watch self pity…
Docile and polite, hum the odd ditty.

MAELSTROM

Two nations apart, they talk, they parley
Try to recall their destinies entwined.
Reeling from their wounds and looking queerly,
They stagger back, aware the beach is mined.
Ante-bellum West is gone, story shined –
High gloss and untouchable, out of reach,
On the very brink of poisoning each…
Their cultures are fraught, serious complaint;
It's time to scrabble about for a leech.
Attempt for a separate peace is just a feint,
But the wreckage needs more than nails and paint.
Stand down to sulfuric state, fear it…
After midnight presence of the spirit.

ALWAYS THE CHARMER

A dumb monster reaches out – slashed back quick.
(What's the feature, have the trailers started?)
The days are twisted and glazed steamy sick,
Score an assumed name, shreaky soul scarred red.
Hot and sour soup becomes the purest cure,
The steam shows a barely thought-out moment,
The abyss-creating events *de jour*.
Sad days, no new rebellion to foment.
Arguably not the man for the job,
Unsuited for this or that, outlook grim.
Bolt the keep to the castle here's the mob,
Screaming murderous rage, make the lights dim.
  While we wait, trash my character some more,
  Always the charmer; oops, there goes the door.

SWAN'S SONG

I had to go to Paris to speak French
I drank the water and suffered the cramp.
Days behind and days ahead, thirst to quench,
There's more to dissemble, becomes the tramp…
Hobo wandering to the blankest beat,
Stone soup for dinner, where're the village folk?
Where will I be when the storm comes to greet,
To explain and soothe, rains narcotic cloak.
I confess I dwell on coffins unbuilt;
Channeled once in kicking up a racket
Or picking up a racquet – time well kilt.
These offenses are ever my jacket.
  I'm myself, foul bird, nesting wherever,
  Up late, down deep, tangled lines to sever.

A NEW HOPE

In the moments following, time has its own way,
The scenery flattens as though a dimension is lost,
A quiet roar is born somewhere deep within and
Emerging, it echoes out all the deafening possibilities.

It takes forever to claw and climb out, your
Own body imprisons, your self so severely
Considering every last implication pending
Sorrow infinite, too much self-pity for dinner.

If you stop moving you'll sink, into a
Finally night darkness, exhausted and weak
The dreams you dreaded no longer fully potent,
Speak out loud, once and future, to tomorrow.

To sunshine, which is certain and forever,
And your best gift, no strings attached ever,
Warming, and nourishing, banishing another
Night to moments that have indelibly happened.

IF MY HEART COULD BEAT

Tonight

Is fallen
Around
My ears, my earnings

To dream

Is full of
Aching
Made easy, made eerie

To belie

Is futile
Alive
Most every, most edgy

Tomorrow

Is fulgurous
Ancient
Misty eaves, misty eyes

THE GODDESS FACTOR

<u>The Real Question Is:</u>

Do I savor the wine from the navel of a goddess

Or do I sorely wallow, a knave in the gutter?

It's a one hundred year-old story heroically told,
Often miscast,
Technicolor themes and a hero redeemed

Then sacrificed.

"For his goddess?" the gathered children ask breathlessly.

<u>Overboard?</u>

Maybe. The mists of dreams and hyperbole
Abound
In my homeland

~Continued~

(Plans and mergers spread out
Lasciviously across the desk)

Attraction is an element of beauty
The goddess is of that beauty, among so many others

And who doesn't want to be a goddess?

<u>Be That As It May...</u>

Overboard?

Yes, all right, you win.

I surrender my pencil
And self

My heresy is my chocolate
Here is my tongue
Do with it what you will.

<u>And In The End.</u>

Retired and exiled
A would-be hero in a convict colony
He drifts slowly through the sunscape

~Continued~

Exotic flora and fauna
To softly adulate

And a part of himself
That is always
The goddess.

I'LL NEVER BE CURED*

Suddenly –

No guide, no one to direct or advise
No shelter, so out there in the cold

What would the streaks of this sunset
     Foretell…

Where I'm sitting is where
I dream we're kissing

Body to body, celestial baby
Yours fits so well in mine

The emptiest arms are mine tonight
With a hunger that beggars

A full moon is a water-lover's time
Looking out with the glow

Understanding back, the reflection
     And the nature

* And I don't much care

MY EVERY EFFORT

Nearer the beach
My friend
Freer than each
My lover

My deepest fantasy
Splashed out
By candlelight in
Our winter hotel

Levitate
Over
Vast
Everywhere
Yell
Our
Ultimate
Return
Animate
Such
Stories

Dizzy and frightened
Neophyte distraught
Distract me chronic chump
Negotiable bounty,
"Libidinous boy, frisk her"

~Continued~

Hush-hush froth
Hunger the
Frowzy hurricane

Specifically stated goals
Position prevailed
During the months of July
Wild and savage
Swallowed…

Desperate sometimes, I
See myself a witless
Incompetent
Chance of success minimal

The punishment becomes punk
Out there the middle ages
We'll never need a microwave
I'll say I was a craftsman

Laying gold leaf
Dedications to my goddess
Never living my crow's-nest crush
Perfect off the script

I don't make real plans
My nakedness shows
Rain like laughter, laughter like rain
I'll blush in the sand, watch the sun

I SHOULD SHUT UP

I know the plan is elaborate – complicated
Mustn't sing awful ejaculate, no potent omen,
No jackdaw shadow on the jalousie.
I might migrate – can't imagine without, a midsummer's
     Anniversary,
We'll walk in the sand and sun again, seduce me
Again, in a crowd where I'm posingly.
I'll slip my stuff in your self-addressed envelope.

I know the tale is primordial – elemental
Get out and thumb! The primrose path is open,
Seek shelter from this hurricane of hubris.
Ignore the mournful *charge d'affaires* this wretched
     Charnel house…
I sense in my sleep where skin touches my waistband,
Imprinting elastic, pale and yielding.
I call in my sleep thinking your fingers to wander.

~Continued~

I know the scheme is hopeless – pie in the sky
God! A hot-blooded tryst tonight, a fuel-soaked
Rag, a suspect device wholly suspensory.
Organdy skirt lightly warbles an oriole's song in
      The woods,
Elusive, barely dressed dryad, tempting
And so gloriously enchanting
Whispering late secrets while you drowse.

THE SEARCHERS

He's shivering in the moonlight
The porch light too
Afraid people will tell him, "You idiot kid"
One last glass though, one last dream…
Where she's been softly treading
He follows trying to catch up

He searches everywhere, even likely
Spots for an answer, a hint
For the needle, must squint
Maybe it's in the snow
Like his car keys once

He visions a knight on a quest
All his sport played carrying
A lady's token (her panties)
Later, from his deserted isle
He re-waltzes every dance; ghost
Sparks of deeply remembered touch

Slippery little devil, if only
He could just hold it for a moment
Unbelievable freaky truth
Everyone crazy and erratic
And hungering for the elusive

I KNOW

Even beneath your sleepy voice,
 Perfectly fragile crumbling Creole,
With 98 out of 100 perfect sounds
 Given to me, as I race wild into the
Black

Tuning in like a maniac, stretching out,
 I'm absolutely connected, then
Into the land of vanishing whispers,
 Half-heard, well-known promises,
Goodnights

Later trying to hurtle a mountain,
 The threads well attached and sending
Good rock steady, electricity on his soul,
 Even long after, of course,
I know

HOPELESSLY

The moonlight shows the Camellia blossoms falling
Plump, pink pillows
Tumbling through
The dark green leaves

In London one night, we're natives now
Hopelessly
A knee-trembler, the wall
Smooth against your back

(Many excuses and stories shot
I'm not here nor am I there
Supposed to be where I'm not
It's likely I'm in the air)

Small secrets are lagniappes
Delightful, lifting me into our dream
Where is the oneiromancist to give hope?
Days to count, I'm sick with desire
And hungering for the elusive…

(El Kabong, he was a hero horse
With a guitar and a mask
Secret identity of course
Loves justice, one has to ask?)

~Continued~

If it costs a million dollars, a flight around the world
Through the minefields
Of a corner of Kosovo,
Or a hellphone on the verizon

A moonless beach beneath the stars
Listening for the echo, when the quiet
Avalanches the night or endless fantasy
Beneath the small Camellia tree

GODDESS DAYS AFAR

Sometimes eerie
Desire at hand
Profound
Crossing boundaries
Landscape

Inescapable
Deftly drawn pure
Parameters
Contact contagious
Feverish

Yes, Baby
Whatever the question
Loving
Journeys unimaginable
Destined

FOLDING CHAIR

On the beach dreaming
And drinking coffee

He pulls his hat low
To see only the dogs

Pushing his feet through
The sand

Somewhere later is
Her sleepy voice
Her slinky choice

Finally back from
Some foreign land
Some forlorn lamb

So many days between
Airports and nearby hotels

Pushing his feet through
The sand

His late afternoon is simple
Drowsy, maybe

~Continued~

Purely drunk with trying to
Remember the future

He's absolutely there now
Breathing on the phone
Bravely in the face

Certainly these are the times
Breathless in fact
Brought in fast

Pushing his feet through
The sand

DESIRES

I want to show you everything of mine…
Warm winter thick night near the beach
Whispering waves and a sultry sand
(The juice is worth the squeeze)
Avenues and freaky venues inland, but the coast
Of course, each beach totaled less than the shore
We'd hold hands and wear shorts…

And see everything of yours…
Crisply clean, a purifying cold and
Muffling snow beneath the endless black
(We could do it on a bicycle in Harvard Square)
We'd fumble for each other 'neath long dark coats
Each town in New England is a castle, ages
Old with stories lengthening cobble stone streets…

EVERY MOMENT

early missed moments:
motoring long miles together
(for two days)
then that night I didn't see
rum-ripped to the gills
and 18 holes of golf
your ass in wonderful shorts

He stood there
And helped her bra off
The first time

Light blue material/set aside/with care? he
can't/remember/topless/her skin
enchanting/luminous/they kissed and talked/and
kissed/his hands on her back/on fire

They whispered in the dark/in the first room
late/she thought to call/a taxi/and put her clothes
back on/but taxis take forever/and
something/could not escape/this time/this night

He stood there
And helped her bra off
The second time

CRAZY ASS MISSING YOU

Wild longing, pressing thoughts
    Erotic ribbon trails
Tangled throughout my day

A portable kingdom, it more
Than exists in my heart

My heart tomorrow is one day
Less, it's on my fevered mind

Now waiting, parked somewhere
    Dark drifting sunset
Trying to reach into a future/past

It's on your lips, moistened nearly
Softly slipping the tip of your tongue

The tip of hesitant and jumping off
From a spot I could nibble forever

A purple sky, a missed connection
    Always so starved
A hand to touch your skin, a hand

I could drag you away, into long days
 Between stations, my body in your hands

~Continued~

My body in your endless rapture, tie
Me up in the dark bound yours forever

Holding my phone with you at last
    Near midnight we whisper
Scorching, so what are you wearing?

CHEMOLITHOAUTOTROPHIC HYPERTHERMOPHILES

It's like a spinning coin

(In the stomach of a gambler
There is no result, only the never-
Ending rush of possibility)

The New Year dawns insane and
    Exciting, he blows
Kisses to each of their midnights
The New Year still has the memory
    Of her touch on his skin
Already he feels something that aches

It's a goldfish suicide

(Orange senseless or merely
Following his own dreaming-tracks,
Gills sparkling in the sunshine)

He chagrins himself each moment –
    Each emotion toward
His inamorata, berries on her
Fingers and beneath-blanket whispers
    Secrets in the heat
Her sisters are his good fortune

~Continued~

It's the cough of a leopard

(Soft and gentle, a lover's slow
Lick, vague but vibrant essence
Of danger, like hotel stationary)

So quietly they gasp, "don't stop"
Hallway sex or parking lot goodbyes

BLACKBERRY DECEMBER

Blackberry December and he's up all night
    Again, so soon, hurtled back
    From the stars

He aches to return heaven borne
    Frazil ices sloes

Turnstile-counting the days, he google-
    Picks the details of the ethereal
    Earlier December berry blast

Blackberry December so far owned
    By the weather
    Watching first the suffering
Anxious last minute snow flights

And as he dreams those lucky sequences,
    Flawless time
Maybe he'll drift through lacy secrets,
    Fluid tides…

Blackberry December is between trips
    Spellbound
    And hell-bent to return
On her panties were the lucky snowflakes
    Pop art in their terror and
    Monkey wrench

~Continued~

He plans everything the same.
      Unwilling to chance it
      To poke at it for no reason

Hill/hell – she voice mailed....
      Of course he'd call her there,
      Like sneaking a smoke,
Wind-swept by some: boom- chicka-
      Boom pool later understood
      The misunderstood, shouldering the rats

Of course he called her back soonest
      Ignored the mist in his face
      The spooky darkness... as he leaned

Against their hot tub, Blackberry December,
      Who isn't? Except for us:
      In love and terrified, so scared

And unbelievably hooked on beyond the holidays
      Constructions and soft
      Blood lines, although he still inquires

He's driven to prove his earlier provenance
      Sensing awareness
Impossible, sad to say
Cocktails and an elevator –
      The first of many, oh so many...

AN UNIVERSAL WOLF

In his stomach
He keeps sheep's eyes
Trying to digest
Golden vision
On pins and needles
He leaves his sleeping
Hopeful, watching
Old sheets of newspaper
Forlornly wafting
On the winter breeze
All day, all-overish,
Who is completely known
Thankfully forgiven?

BEAUTIFUL AND WONDERFUL

It's believing, or relishing
An insatiate thirst, a tyrant
Sparing none... he imagines,
A heavenly mermaid in the bay
He produces minor works
Styling himself a celebrant

Echo late no more, words that absorb
    The sparse sanity
He'll emulate a bore, rapidly repeating
    Yellow journalism
Shoot estimate none, nor look for
    A little, overwrought systems
Sad educate before, like unruly class-
    Mates, they go bare-chested

All his monomania is envisioned
On a boat alone for years– let go now,
Like Richie's falcon
Or stories from the report – let go then,
Like Margo's finger
He thinks he knows the difference
Between polenta and placenta
(It's how you cook it)

He plans to be a transient for 800 years
Her life over his transparent yet unshed tears
Hell yes, life is transitory, god save their fears

A TENDENCY, ATENDENCY

But the words are so beautiful…
Rampant echolalia blankets
Inside his head –keeping warm
The flush, slightly
A more ashamed fool

He resolves and re-resolves…
Go easy boy, you
Lay your tongue out there
An outright laugher – wildly
Intoxicating boots all over

Yet fingers dial again unhesitatingly…
Ever, he's an open book
He thinks he must breathe
Tomorrow he'll so boldly
Reiterate like a slug

YOUR SISTER FALLS ASLEEP
WITH THE TV ON

This is my baby,
Whispered in the dark
Given like a dream
Tangled fast for now

Yes, we have to say
Right now
Your legs with mine
Together unbelievable

One last thought:
Back to the sun and the beach
One side, we hide
We're up so late…

We'll stay young forever
Your nails on my thighs
Triple my dreams and
You're not even close

HOSTAGE SITUATION

The artwork was violent and pop
Full of bright colors like green and
Orange: I held it just this way.
"Do you like this?" I asked,
Knowing she wouldn't – artists are
The worst critics. There was a light
Puncture wound in my palm. A small
Point of blood escaped and
Fell onto the upper left corner.

An ice cream man at night beneath
The neon can't make a sale and the music
Doesn't make a difference. Some suits and
Glittery dress, lizard-like on the board-
Walk, watch with not a little amusement,
Sipping stuff and being serene. He parks his
White truck and heads for the beach –
Nips a little vodka and sucks an orange
Popsicle, sits in the sand, in the green dark.

At five I leave the shop,
The shaded alley beautiful, then turn the corner
Into the sun blazing across three
Consecutive parking lots. They are
Lacerated by two very easy streets – light
A cigarette, bob and weave through the
Big old fish trucks, hear sounds
Behind me and turn, she's smoking scary,
And running short steps blind sober.

APPEARANCES I

It was so early in the morning
The streets were only riddled with light
Red bricks of old Prince St. moaned at the hour
Beams slipped through with hints to come.

She and her dog dropped onto Thompson
Both paused, Jugs leapt and ran against his lead
She lit a cigarette and pushed up her sunglasses
Wrapped her coat tighter, pale blonde tiger stripes

Juggernaut was feeling good, warm rested
Restless from breakfast, hours of luxurious sleep
She was the same, sort of impatient but slacking
Tall leather boots scratching behind him dutifully

Spinning on her heel she headed toward
Houston, bearing down briskly in the cold air
Jugs running a bit faster, snorting the world
The church bells rang six o'clock

APPEARANCES II

More than twenty blocks north, in a spare
Well-kept studio off Fifth Ave., a quiet street
Relatively, he thought as he rolled over, why
Had he woken so early? Head ached, mouth dry

He hadn't worked yesterday, instead drinking beer
Watching vacant TV, then on into the long night
One movie after another, he didn't remember
Going to bed, during the Dirty Dozen, he reckoned

He began to imagine his coffee maker working
On its own, ground beans, he could almost see it
Dripping into the glass pot, a cup floated clean
From the cupboard, filled itself, searched for bed

The man in the bed with the blankets pulled up
To his eyes lay there, the studio absolutely silent
Around him – comfortable, embracing tight
Out his ling fugitive initiative -- really

APPEARANCES III

Mickey sat in his patrol car smoking, an hour
And a half left on his shift, 12 to 8, another
Quiet night in the first precinct, he almost missed
His partner even though he hated the man.

He saw her and the little black and white dog
They curved the corner, breath steaming from each
He watched her legs, again, as he had the six days
His partner had been in the hospital.

Mickey'd seen the guy with the bottle, the contents
Seemed to be his, wet red hot, but right behind
His partner, they'd been arguing, Mickey and him,
Faced off, both surprised as the bottle came down.

Of course he'd busted the drunk psycho and called
A bus, the skull was cracked and he was critical,
Mickey went out that next day, got drunk, watched
As women took their clothes off, Times Square.

BLUE LAND

In the history of civilization
Before ideas
The ancient people beguile –
The many gods protect

I try to be like them, not thinking
Of change but blissful constancy

In the city with the wide-eyed glare
Progress fueling upon itself
Grossly susceptible to it
I am all too human

BLUE FIRE

There's a traveler
In a thousand fleshy nights
Who remembers faces; he soldiers bravely
Holding himself to the painful highest
Discarding his physical self in torment

By sunlight he weakens
Hides behind a curtain or door
From all the thighs he's interrupted
There's relief in his luciferous frailty

And yet a fear?

There's a traveler
On self-imposed parade
Through artificial life
Beginning and committing at dark
His unspeakably damp trade
Borne through the streets on weary legs

BLUE WATER

What a cool character the mother was!
A lithe personality
In the lives of those around

She was admired from the blatant depths
Of Belfast and beyond, though she never knew
Yet in the idol is the deep –

Mystery of the unknown woman

BLUE SKY

Every day is not a promise
Some will always evade

There's treasure out the window
When all the city drowses
Certain breaking sounds creep in
Like agents in stealth
And the virgin in heart

They finally please to sleep
The last fearful watchers

CRIME

She put a cigarette in his mouth
And her nails were very red
This was in the kitchen and they leaned
Against the counter smoking some words

Her legs were trim black lines
Her sad expression spoke ill of the city
She wore a beautiful silk jacket
He talked about liking it, meaning he wanted

～ just to touch her

And he might have reached out wielding a held breath
But she fell into deep quiet and examined the floor
Through her own grey smoke
She was missing as a cake eater was suddenly there

Somehow he knew he had committed
Or had he? Just by thought that hadn't dared
Or intent now separated by trees of free
Men and women, landscape imperfect with the face

～ of brutishness

He implored his eyes their shiftiness
Random darting, snatches of her pretend to be
For some reason he remembers her roman nose
And rubs his own in another spasm of treachery

~Continued~

    Her head bends to pour more wine
    He dreams, white fingers
    And take-out food
    He had strayed
    Off, in some wrong
    Land
    It felt awfully unlawful
    But he really couldn't
    Better
    The second
    He saw:
    Two live butterflies
    Black motions just barely
    Mesmerizing
    A thousand common
    Objects
    Began to illuminate
    And canonize

He reached his arm around her shoulder
Snagging a few long black hairs
Glimpses of the future can be horribly potent
His hand touched a skinny shoulder reaching

Like a silver cloth with infinite folds
Crossed with even more thin black threads

~Continued~

As every moment of her was crossed with him
Which fingers finally grazed in wonder at

~ that white skin?

The bells at the church rang
Maybe six months earlier, where threads
Hadn't crossed: his finger were incomplete

(Love's a wonderful thing, Son)
Somebody somewhere on the upside
Of a feeling like flannel incline, separately
Creeping back, god the violence committed

The strains of some ancient opera humming desperately
Her shoulder was lean, but soft
Under her silk blouse blushing beneath
A drunken re-examination and recantation, he suffers

~ her pained look in multiple scenes

AFTERWORD

I wore red sleeves and more
A man sat alone
In a hat store
Brightly colored they
Hung everywhere.

I didn't go in at all
The sleeves would become
Me
For the chi-chi shop
Though I stood and looked

I guess no one was yet
Buying hats just
For Christmas and winter
When these I wore
Would be fairly clashing.

www.ingramcontent.com/pod-product-compliance
Lightning Source LLC
Chambersburg PA
CBHW022007100426
42738CB00041B/859